KALEIDOSCOPE

KARI THOMASON

Books by KARI THOMASON

Kaleidoscope

Books Available on Lulu.com
Amazon, and Barnes & Noble

Contact Information:

FB address:
https://www.facebook.com/kari.thomason.3781

Email:
karithomason02g.mail.com

Contact Information for
WILDFIRE PUBLICATIONS:

wildfire.publications@hotmail.com

DEDICATION
BY Kari Thomason

To my children – Shane and Trudi and 3 grandsons - Ben, Max and Phoenix, who stayed with me throughout my journey.

TABLE OF CONTENTS

JOURNEY

Picking Up The Bottle

I had my first drink when I was 9 years old
I was brought up in a Roman Catholic Children's Home
After being abused by a Priest, one of the nuns
Caught me burying my blood-stained knickers
I was marched up to the Staff bathroom
Where I was whipped on my bare bottom and the
Backs of my legs with a rubber hose pipe
I was then locked in the Chapel to say sorry to God
Dinner time went. Tea time went. They had forgotten me
I ate the Communion and drank all the Alter Wine
It made the pain go away
At 13 I was raped by my Foster Father
I picked up the bottle
It made the pain go away
At 16 I met a man who constantly beat me
I picked up the bottle
It made the pain go away
Fifteen years ago, my Husband (A good man)
Committed suicide
I picked up the bottle
It made the guilt go away
I am now a Carer for my Partner
Who is terminally ill
A different kind of pain
I NO longer pick up the bottle
I pick up the PHONE

I have just reached my 12-month Anniversary

<u>Your Best Friend</u>

The journey you are on
May take awhile
You will find it hard
To accept a smile
When you are weak
We will be strong
We'll give you strength
To carry on
You were our cement
When the rockery cracked
Trust our love
To guide you back
Remember our dreams
We built with care?
With lots of love
And more to spare
I will kiss your wounds
I'll help you mend
As your wife, your lover
Your best friend

The Light

I saw you I couldn't reach you
You had built a wall
Only you could break
You struggled
couldn't free you
Just one small step
Only you could take
I saw your despair
Your soul was searching
Felt your pain, it was so real
The scars were there
Your wounds were weeping
I hoped and prayed
That you would heal
There was a light, you couldn't see it
An Angel stood so very near
Your heart was begging
Your eyes were pleading
Show me the light
Through the ear
There is a light
We'll keep it burning
Your Soul will flourish
For you are good

And all the time
We will be learning
To accept your peace
Once we have understood
BE FREE

<u>Needs</u>

A bird needs air to fly in
A flower it needs rain
A daughter needs her mother
To help console her pain
A puppet it needs winding
A cut it needs a stitch
A duckling it needs guiding
From falling in a ditch
Lovers don't need magic
To make their future bright
Dreamers they need silence
To dream all through the night
Two people they need courage
Yes, it does take two
To say just only three small words
I NEED YOU

<u>Stop, Think, Remember</u>

Times are bleak
And you're feeling low
Don't know what to do
Or where to go?
Stop and think
Think carefully now
Think of others
Another murder?
A child with no mother
The heartache of parents
Their child is missing
Killings in Ireland
Bombs still hissing
Children that are starving
And are sure to die
They'll never get the chance
To ask the world "Why".
Remember, each step you take
Others may never walk
Each complaint you make
Remember, others may never talk
Each flower you pick
Remember, others will never see
For all the animals caged
Remember, you are FREE

Is Anyone There?

Hello, can you hear me?
Is there anyone there?
I'm in a dark, dark place
I'm huddled, cold and small
I don't know if I'm awake
I don't think that I'm asleep
Would it make a difference it I cry?
Would it make a difference if I speak?
Can I curl into a small, small ball?
Children and pets play with balls
They throw them high, so high
Yes, let's go there
Up to the sky
Sway with the feather light kites
Hold tight to their pretty ribbons
Huff to encourage the wind
To keep you safe
From the forbidden
Hello, can you hear me?
Is there anyone there?
It won't hurt so much
Won't be too hard to bear
As long as I know someone
Will be there.......after
To give me a cuddle
All I want is a CUDDLE

Tears Fall Slowly

Tears fall slowly
They just won't stop
Thinking of what I had
Thinking of what I've got
I had a voice
I had a choice
The path I chose
To others was wrong
Just like the words
In a pathetic love song
Tears fall slowly
On barren ground
Plenty of excuses
To be found
I had two beautiful children
I was a wife
I had a loving husband
Who ended his life
He loved me more
Than words could say
I couldn't love back
He couldn't stay
Tears fall slowly
And they will last
How can I live in the future?
When I died in the past?

<u>My Special Place</u>

There's a special place
I like to go
When I feel confused
When I'm feeling low
When I'm feeling lost
Vulnerable and bare
A place I go
Where all is fair
A special place
That gives 'safe ' hugs
Where butterflies
Chase away the bugs
Where children are praised
When they are good
Encouraged to be free
never misunderstood
Where children are safe
Warm and fed
Only happy thoughts
Inside their heads
Where there are lots giggles
Cuddles too
Those magic words
"I Love You"
A special place
Inside my mind
Lots of beautiful flowers
Many many kinds

Where rainbows stretch
So so far
Nothing but laughter
Can be heard from afar
A special place
Only I know
Where I can escape
Where I can grow
Where I am SAFE

When

God, I'm so angry
From deep within I guess,
When did life get so hard?
When did I get so depressed?
Where has all the laughter gone?
The tomorrows and the smiles
All that is left is loneliness
Each step an empty mile
A wife, a sister, a mother
Surely that should be enough?
Then why do I feel so frightened?
And confused when faced with love.
Is it love that is the reason?
I wish I could see what they see,
Everything they love and like
When all there is, is ME

When

I look in the mirror
What do I see?
A total stranger
Staring back at me
There is no smile
Her eyes are red
Should you read her mind
She wishes she was dead
Silent and crying
A lost lingering stare
Just another mirror
Just another cross to bear
She polishes the mirror
Expecting a change
But the face in the mirror
Remains the same
She's hurt all those around her
She's hurt all that are close
She wishes she could stop
Those she has hurt the most
HER CHILDREN

Look

Look into my mind
An empty space,
Look into my soul
An empty place
Look into my heart what do you see?
Look closer now,
Look carefully.
There was a place
As a child,
When things were crazy
When things were wild.
A place I'd go
To play hide and seek
They would look and look
I would hide and weep.
A mirror without glass
An envelope without a seal
Look again, my friend
This is real.

<u>Hurt</u>

I'm a little girl
Running free
I'm a small child
Sat on his knee
The child soon went
No longer free
That was when he hurt me
My tears didn't
Didn't tell me
I was sad
My tears only
Told me
I was BAD
The blood and the pain
He could clearly see
That was when
He hurt me
I'm a Teenager now
With a dark past
They offered me love
The love didn't last
Part of a family
I'm not meant to be
That was when he hurt me
I'm an adult now
A job not well done
Seems only sadness
No smiles no fun

A Normal person
I'm not meant to be
That is why
I HURT ME

<u>No One's Street</u>

There is a street called No One's Street
Where rich people didn't go
Only people doing their jobs
We're the people who wanted to know
Still, they had to earn a living
To live in their fancy homes
To drive around, in their big posh cars
Down the street, where no one was known
Kids lived in run down houses
With Windows boarded up
No pennies for the new glass
No cupboards full of love
Smoke never came out of their chimneys
On a bitter winter's night
Candles, they were all some had
Their heating and their light
Then came the night of the storm
When every kid knew fear
In number 14, a little girl sat
Wishing her Mummy was near
Her legs and feet, arms, were bare
Her dress was dirty and torn
Her nose was runny, her eyes Huge
From hunger and forlorn
BANG BANG BANG the board moved
She let out one big scream
'Jack Frost' had come to get her
His eyes so big and green

Now the letterbox was talking
How did it know her name?
Maybe he'd chase 'Jack Frost' away?
The cat, now in from the rain
"Don't be frightened Angel
Just do as I ask
Stand on your tiptoe, try reach the key
My, you are a clever lass...."
She tried and tried, but couldn't reach
Sobbing with despair
Wee wee trickled down her legs
She'd be in trouble, no more spare
Then the loudest scream, she'd ever screamed
Came from out of her mouth
As two strong arms, picked her up
And was shouting something out aloud
"It's ok Angel, don't be afraid
I'm going to take you somewhere safe
That's right Little One, hold on tight
Let's get you out of this place".
Would he find Mummy?
Chase away 'Jack Frost' at last?
She didn't want the sweeties now
The pennies would buy new glass
Outside blue lights were flashing
Lots of people standing around
Shocked whispers, some angry shout
Her own whimpering muffled sounds
The new house was big
Her new friend was nice
Out of No One's Street at last
Tucked up in a warm bed
She said her prayers
And thanked God
All the Windows had GLASS

<u>A Rainy Day</u>

Angels are crying, up in the sky
There's lots of confusion
WHY? WHY? WHY?
Do the clouds have the answer
Have they had their fill?
No more rain can they hold
SPILL SPILL SPILL
My eyes are misty
My cheeks are wet
My heart is shouting
LET LET LET
Me HEAL
Just another rainy day

A Fair Deal

Don't look at me
If you don't give a Damn
I won't walk away
I will play my hand
Win or lose
The cards are there
Do I take the risk?
Do I really care?
Am I the Joker
Of the pack?
A Poker face
Do I lack?
Aces and Kings
Fives and Tens
Shuffle the pack
Let's begin again
Win or lose
What the hell
Queen of Hearts
My story will tell

<u>Look At Me</u>

Look at me
What do you see?
An aggressive person
Or a confident me?
Is my head held low?
Eyes to the ground,
Or is my head held high
Justice to be found?
Look at me
Pretend that you care
Hear my voice
A voice from nowhere
Do the shrinks have the answer?
Medication they give
Swiftly moving on to the next
Will they die?.......Will they live?
You have a choice
Please listen to me
Please, please hear my voice
LOOK AT ME!

Our Joe

There is someone I've never talked about
My big brother, Our Joe
A story waiting to be told
From 25 years ago
Please bear with me
This may be hard to write
But God is telling me
The time is now right
Our Joe was my Hero
When we were growing up
He would take the beatings
When he wouldn't let me own up
A chocolate bar for 20 pence
Why did they beat him?
To a 6-year-old, it didn't make sense
Our Joe was hungry
The chocolate I did nick
I thought no one was looking
I thought that I'd been quick
The police were called
Our Joe said, "Keep it shut"
I had a telling off
They kicked his butt
They took us home
Drank tea with the Nuns
Already in our hearts
The fear had begun
I didn't see Our Joe

For the next 2 days
I couldn't even recognise his face
They told the hospital
He had fallen down the stairs
"You know how clumsy boys can be......"
Even I knew at 6,
It wasn't the stairs
If I spent my Collection money
On sweets, like kids do
He would give me his bus fare
Telling me off, but grinning too
Then he'd walk the 3 miles home
So, in trouble, I wouldn't get
Heading for another beating
Was a sure bet
Every Sunday, with a Priest
He would disappear
To the Laundry building
He never showed me his fear
Then one day, he was grown
Old enough to go to Sea
Our Joe, my Protector
He had left me
He would come when he could
To take me out for the day
Oh, what fun we had
I would beg him to stay
He'd question me all the time
Have any of them hurt you?
I'd lie, and say I'm fine
Years went by and we lost touch
He was kicked out of the Navy
Oh, I missed him so much
Then came the call, from my dad
In my heart of hearts
I knew it was bad

Our Joe had hung himself
For me, a note he did leave
The bastards have won
But Little One, please be live
God will take care of you
He will help you find your way
It is too late for me I just cannot stay
I'm heading for the FIRES
They really taught us well
Be strong, my Little One
Don't let them get you as well
I have hurt many people
Mind, body and Soul
That is why I must go
What hurts the most
Is your love and Faith in me?
I'm not your Hero Little One
I'm a COWARD, don't you see?
PLEASE, PLEASE, PLEASE
Don't cry for me

As a child, I often watched him
He always looked so sad
He was lost, confused and angry
Our Joe, my Hero

<u>Sundays...Past</u>

God, I hate Sundays
They say your day of rest
What happens to the rest of the week?
When I am put to the test?
I wake up every morning
Wishing I wasn't here
Waiting for your instructions
Loud and Clear
You have taken all my family
Leaving me behind
I guess you had your reasons
Answers I can't find
Oh God, I am hurting
The pain I cannot bear
Please, please give me a sign
To show me that you're there
Lift the weight of my shoulders
Ease the pain in my Heart
Please, please strengthen my Faith
Help me make a fresh start

TURNING POINT

Sundays....Present

God, I LOVE Sundays
It's true, your day of rest
Well deserved, coping with me all week
I hope I passed each test?
I wake up every morning
Thanking you, that I am here
Waiting for your instructions
To come Loud and Clear
Yes, you had taken all my family
Leaving me behind
I couldn't understand your reasons
The answers you helped me find
God, I am no longer hurting
The pain I no longer bare
It has taken me a lot of years
To realise you're not going anywhere
You have lifted the weight
Of my shoulders
Filled the emptiness in my heart
God, I LOVE Sundays
Each one a fresh start

You Wouldn't Go Away

I've shouted, I've sighed
I've laughed I've frowned,
I have predicted
You would let me down
Yeah, yeah, yeah
I've heard it all before
Save your breath
I know the score.
But you wouldn't go away.
For every question
An answer you had,
Some hard to swallow
Some even sad
Some very confusing
But they opened a door,
You had my attention
I wanted to know more.
Did you think I wasn't interested?
Curious, I was in fact
But we speak different languages
Like a game of tit for tat
But you wouldn't go away.
Did you see me as a know all?
I call it freedom of speech.
Did you see me as unapproachable?
Too hard to reach
Some see me amusing,
Downright cocky: to some extent.

Impatient, very tiresome
To all-purpose and intent
But you wouldn't go away.
Each time I turned away from you
You would whisper in my ear
"I have enough patience for the both of us"
My call, I know you hear.
So many doors have been slammed on you
But mine is opened wide,
No longer will you walk behind
But right here by my side.
I will not go away.
Every hand that I have dealt you
You have taken on the chin,
"Come my child, let me carry you
Free you from your sin"
Thank you for not going away
For choosing my soul to save,
I'll proudly walk the path you chose for me
The path that you have paved

I'd Like To Say

I'd like to say
I'm doing all right
I'd like to say
I'm doing fine
I'd like to say
All is how it should be
I'd like to say
Just a matter of time
I'd like to say
That I'm not struggling
I'd like to say
My Faith is in tact
I'd like to say
A whole lot of things
I'd like to say
Enough of that
I'd like to say
That I am not doubting
I'd like to say
I am not afraid
I'd like to say
That I could make more effort
Each and every time I prayed
I'd like to say
That I am not lonely
I'd like to say
I am not in pain
I'd like to say

That I have the strength
To believe all over again
I'd like to say
I know he hears me
I'd like to say
Won't he help me, so?
I'd like to say
Show me a signpost
I'd like to say
Which way do I go?
I'd like to say
My heart is open
Please don't leave it bare
I'd like to say
God has spoken
To tell me that he cares
I'd like to say....

<u>Overworked Angel</u>

I say goodnight to you
Every night
Your name is the first on my lips
At dawn's first light
It has been seven years
Since you went away
With all my heart
I wanted you to stay.
If I'm having a bad day
I ask you to make it better
If there is no post
I ask you for a letter
If it's raining hard
I ask you to make it stop
Just until I get home
Or back from the shop.
If my heart is heavy
Or my mood is low,
I ask you for directions
Which way should I go?
Many loved ones have passed
Over all the years
Yet it is you I ask

To calm my fears
No more demands
No more tests,
I can finally
Put you to rest.
SISTER...I LOVE YOU

A Smile

I smiled today
Followed by a frown
My spirits are high
Should they not be down?
Enter confusion
Followed by despair
Yet the face in the mirror
Says I don't really care
Is that right?
Is that wrong?
It's such a long time
Since you've been gone
I have travelled mile after mile
A Soul-Searching journey
To find a smile
Lord please let me hold onto it
Please let it last
For more than a moment
Let me keep my new happiness

Broken Chains

You broke the chains
That bound me
To you, my life I give
For you have set me free
Giving me hope to live
I begged, I screamed I hollowed
There was no way out
Despair had already got me
But you had heard my shout
The prison that held me
Was in my mind and my heart
The chains so tightly bound me
No strength to pull them apart
You sought me in the darkness
Saw my tears and pain
You came to my rescue
Breaking all my chains
You came to me in the night
The time I dread the most
I felt your arms around me
I felt as warm as toast
One by one the chains were gone
A future I now had with hope
Mountains, hills whatever
Now I knew that I would cope
My mind you are leaving open
My eyes and ears as well
So, I can see and hear others

Who are chained and imprisoned in hell
My open heart now bursting
With overwhelming love, to you I give
My heart, Soul and Spirit
Are yours as long as I live

Lord   I am forever yours

<u>My Pen</u>

Pen in hand
Page is bare
Can't seem to find the words
I just sit and stare
I need a release
I need an escape
Yet, here I sit
Pen, no mark it makes
My heart is heavy
My eyes are full
Maybe my pen
Needs a refill?
My thoughts are jumbled
Scattering here and there
Aiming, nowhere in particular
Just darkness and despair
I'm trying to get a grip, to this old, old song
I could change the lyrics I could change the tune
Soul searching aimlessly
It's not time it's too soon
God, if you're listening
I need help with this task
I'm strong but I'm tired
I'm in a real mess
Please guide my pen
To fill out this page
A release from the anger
A release from the cage

?????

I am sat in my kitchen
A sadness descends
Like a ball of wool
I can't find the ends
Trying to unravel my thoughts
Just like the ball of wool
There's something niggling
Pull.   Pull. Pull
I pick up my pen
Start a new page
The words struggle to come
Calmness, no rage
My life is good at the moment
A lot to embrace
So where is my head at the moment?
I don't like this place
Round and around in circles I go
What am I missing?
What don't I know?

Why am I sat in silence?
Trying to go it alone
When his presence is here
I am not my own
He always listens
He never turns away
He is always there
Even when my prayers go astray

I am smiling now
And singing out loud
By the volume of the music
You'd think there was a crowd
God has filled my heart
He has filled my Soul
Never again to stop talking to him
Now are my utmost goals

Should

Two new inhalers
Along with a new pill
Terrific! Yet another
Prescription to fill
You should see an improvement
Oh, really? I should?
Why give them
In the first place
If you didn't think I would?
You should do more exercise
You should lose weight
Should, should, should
Grrrrrr that word I hate
You should try stay positive
You should listen
To what I say
You should keep all appointments
You should make your own way
You should do this
You should do that
They could take SHOULD
Out of his vocabulary
And replace it with PAT
A pat on the head
Being treated like a kid
Nodding and promising
To do as he bid

Well, it has been a week
And I really must say
There has been improvement
In a positive way
Yes, there it is
I'm feeling good
Maybe it's not that negative
That little word SHOULD

Steps

Little steps
Small steps
Slow steps
Don't be in such a rush
That's all I seem to hear
Be patient
God has a plan for you
All will become clear
Here I am, willing
Able, and waiting
To follow God's new Plan
But I've never been growth patience
I hope God understands?
Little steps
Small steps
Steady steps
Isn't it good that I AM keen?
Why can't it begin, like tomorrow?
I don't think that's what he means
When the time is right
As you grow
You will have answers
You will know
I really must try
My impatience to curb
By taking
Little steps
Small steps

Kari Thomason/Kaleidoscope

Steady steps
And wait patiently
For his WORD

Yet Again

2.58 am another sleepless night
Only the darkness for company
Yawning, getting as mad as hell
Yet again, sleep evades me
Is it my thoughts, whizzing around?
Or my aches and pains
This night, that keeps me awake?
Perhaps, it's the noise of the odd eerie sounds
I can imagine, the picture my face makes?
I have tried counting sheep
As always, I've prayed
Done riddles, inside my head
I've turned to pen and paper
Which usually works
I am asleep usually, before I reach the zzzzzzzzz

<u>Dear Lord</u>

Don't take me yet
It is way too soon
I've too much to do
Before my journey to the moon
There are plans to be made
More healing to be done
Especially with
My daughter and Son
My life has been interesting
If that's the right word
The only one I can think of
And a million times heard
I could have done some things
Better
But so could you
A lot of pain and sorrow
You put me through
I know you had your reasons
Each lesson a test
With my faith still in tact
I have come out the best
I feel I have been lucky
I have been blessed
But there is one thing
I need to confess
I won't be coming quietly
But, pain free I hope
I'm Starting to wonder

If you'll be able to cope
I will be singing my heart out
New lungs will be mine
Dancing up the stairway
No more arthritis, new spine
A young healthy bladder
No Tena Lady's in sight
No 'Spec Saver' glasses
Just perfect eyesight
Yes, I will arrive
Perfect, brand new
And the rest as they say
"Is up to you".

Answers

I have come to Church
To feel closer to God
I think he may have gone AWOL?
Happy, smiling faces greet me
All I want to do is brawl
What's wrong with me God?
What am I doing wrong?
I'm up and down, like a yo-yo
Am I being tested God?
My fears, are they a no-no?
It's Wednesday today I attend
Normally on a Sunday
Everyone seems to know everyone
Perhaps, because its Wednesday?
The tears are flowing
I can't make them stop
But neither, can I understand why?
Should they ask?
What would be my reply?
God! Give me something
A sign, a gesture......what?
Anything to let me know
That I'm not losing the plot
I still have my Faith God
But I'm struggling, bad
Believe me, I'm really trying
Am I putting in 100%?
If I'm unsure, is that classed as lying?

Is eaten here, in disguise?
Surely, they wouldn't let him in?
Don't let him get within
An inch of my life
I will stop my questions
I will dry my tears
I won't cause anyone else this strife
God, is in the building I have been told
Sat right beside me, my hands he holds
Yes, he knows that I'm struggling
He says that is ok
With his precious love, again he reassures me
That with me, he is here to stay

<u>Sinking But Not Drinking</u>

God! Another test?
When will they stop?
I am 16 months dry
Haven't touched a drop
So many tests
So far, I've passed them all
Why is this one
Making me fall?
I've done my soul searching
I have shed my tears
I have called on my faith
That has got me through the years
Yet I am sinking
Sinking so fast
Deep down I go
Beneath the grass
Through the soil
Cold and dry
It's in my mouth
It's in my eye
Lower and lower
Deeper I go
Can't see the bottom
Do I want to, though?
HEY! Wait a second
Time to rewind
I've just re-read the last verse
Too much to leave behind

I look in each hand
No can or bottle there
So, what is the cause
Of this sudden despair
People have given me friendship
They have given me praise
They seem to genuine like me
Of which I'm amazed
Could this test be emotional?
The thing I find hard to accept
The big one called LOVE
For a battered heart......and yet
The scars are fading
Might make me raw and mew
All I ask please be patient
As I climb my way back up to you

Roller Coaster

I'm on a roller coaster
One I don't want to get off
If you had met me
16 months ago
I would have begged
Make the bugger stop
Stop the world from turning
Spinning out of control
No light at the end of the bottle
Only one place
I was sure to go
Until that day I looked into the mirror
The image, it seemed to speak
"Who do you see?
Looking at you?
A girl, a woman, a freak?"
Someone so so tired
Someone nearly on her knees
Someone silently begging
Won't you help me please
Today I am looking in the same mirror
The image, again does speak
"Wow! Hey looking good,"
From another healthy week
In fact, it's been a healthy year
Your eyes are clear and bright
Your heart is full
Your liver good

Not a can or bottle in sight
Yes! This is one roller coaster
Where I am enjoying the ride
Some twists and turns
A few bumps here and there
But I am in control of the ride

<u>Can't</u>

Can't someone see past my illness?
Can't someone show that they care?
Can't someone take me on a journey
Full of magic, no despair
Can't someone be non-judgemental?
Can't someone lean to like my smile?
Can't someone be willing?
To go that extra mile
Can't someone accept my sense of humour?
Can't someone, with happiness, make me sigh?
Can't someone be always on stand by
To hold me when I cry
Can't someone fill in the emptiness?
Can't someone fill the gap?
Can't someone find my heart in the darkness?
Without needing to use a map
Can't someone make me laugh again?
Can't someone want to take the chance?
Can't someone fill, my life once more
With laughter, love and romance

<u>Hitting The Spot</u>

I have a big spot
On my nose
It's right in the centre
And it just grows
As plain as day
For everyone to see
It's the first thing they notice
Before they see me
So, this got me thinking
As someone I do
What's the first thing people see
When they see you?
Perhaps your hair?
You forgot to brush
Has a mind of its own?
You were in such a rush
Perhaps your smile?
So bright and wide
Is it a genuine one?
What troubles does it hide?
Perhaps your teeth
If you're lucky to have some
Well, it's all part of the smile
When you greet someone
Perhaps your clothes
Crumpled and not pressed
To go with the hair
That is a total mess

Perhaps your eyes? Windows to the Soul
Do they have a story?
Waiting to be told?
Or do they see the whole you?
Spots and all
Then give them a big Hug
Because they heard your call
They are there

<u>Role Model(s)</u>

Whatever the circumstances
How we entered this world
Be it a tall handsome stranger
Meeting a young Naive girl?
True love, or a crime?
The deed has been done
Who would be classed
Role model number one?
What about the widow
Who lost her husband to the war?
He never got to see
The child she bore
Who grew up to be
An angry young man
No male role model
Is that hard to understand?
What about the addict
Raised in a broken home
Lost his self-respect, home and family
Is he a role model on his own?
How about the 'Perfect family'
Big house, educated kids
Money not an issue
But they have no time to give
Why are all the Text Books?
Obsessed with these words?
A double-barrelled label
Freely given out, I've heard

I believe everyone does
The best that they can
Childhood, school, society
Each of our lives has a plan
If we believed and took notice
To all that was said
Would the elderly live longer?
Would the young get ahead?
Live for today
Yesterdays are gone
Shake off all those labels
It's time to write a new song

<u>Am I?</u>

Am I brave
Am I strong
Am I right
AM I wrong
Am I happy
Am I sad
AM I good
Am I bad
Am I a child
Am I grown
Am I frightened
Am I alone
Am I alive
Am I dead
Am I starving
Am I Fed
Am I a nightmare
Am I unfeeling
Am I incapable
Am I unwilling
Am I a disappointment
Am I a success
Am I even worthy
Of passing this test

<u>DESTINATION</u>

<u>I Am</u>

I am brave
I am strong
I am not always right
I am sometimes wrong
I am happy
I am sometimes sad
I am trying to be good
I am trying not to be bad
I am sometimes a child
I am grown
I am sometimes frightened
I am not ALONE
I am alive
I am not dead
I am not starving
I am fed
I am sometimes a nightmare
I am sometimes unfeeling
I am capable
I am willing
I am not a disappointment
I am a success
I AM going to pass this test

<u>Angels</u>

You came into my life
When there was total despair whether I wanted you or not
You were always there
You listened, thought, saw
And said
With little to go
You still went ahead
You accepted my fears, tears and pain
With nothing to lose
And nothing to gain
With gentle words
And a tender touch
You gave everything
But not too much
There was a light
All be it dim
There was no map
You saw within
The scars are there
for others to feel
You have given me the strength
To help them HEAL

The Main Man

Ok, my heart is wide open
My Soul I do bear
So where is the man
They say is everywhere?
Sure, I know he is busy
Taking care of the world
Couldn't he spare 10 minutes
For a lost, frightened little girl
They say he always listens
That each word is heard
The Shepherd attending his flock
No matter what size the herd?
I have ticked all the boxes
I have done all he has asked
I don't think I am asking
Too big a task?
Am I waiting for a bolt of lightning?
Or even a mere gentle touch
Am I not giving it my all?
Am I expecting too much?
I have always had my faith
Which has always got me through somehow
So, an honest open question
Why am I struggling now?
I'm not asking for a Miracle
A break will do just fine
My heart and Soul I give to you
But sorry God, patience isn't mine.

<u>Teardrop</u>

Teardrop has fallen
But it is confused
By the time it reached my chin
It was totally amused
You see, we've been here before
Many a time
Nursing a broken heart
Or when a poem wouldn't rhyme
A dark, dark place
Small and afraid
When its brothers and sisters
Rolled down my face
Lower than rock bottom
Nowhere else to go
Feeding my misery with the bottle
A way out I don't know

Hey! Back to the Teardrop
The one that's confused
Let me try and explain
Why it was confused?
I feel I have been asleep
For a hundred years
And I have awoken
With joys and cheers
The world looks new
A whole different place
I have the biggest smile

On my face
A feeling in my stomach
I don't recognize
And it has taken me
Totally by surprise
Some may call it harmony
Some may call it calm
Some, even happiness
Like a lucky charm
Do I take out Insurance?
Do I put it under Arrest?
For me and my HAPPY teardrop
Must do our best
This feeling to keep
INNER PEACE

<u>Open Heart Surgery</u>
(A collaboration written by Kari and Alan Kemp)

My heart was broken but I didn't know
It was missing the Power of His life cleansing flow
I carried the weight of this heart of stone
That blocked this vessel as I sailed alone

The storm that raged had swept me away
Yet I didn't realise as I was blinded by the spray
But the Lord loved me and searched my heart
Healing the scars that had set me apart

The miracle He performed made my heart beat again
Giving a testimony of my broken chains
He didn't bypass my soul but gave a second chance
Re directing the streams of life through every circumstance

Each step, he tenderly prepared me
For the surgery that was to take place
Knowing exactly when I was ready
To accept his loving embrace

For years the wounds had been weeping
A barren, unattended site
God gently reached into the darkness
With his Holy, Healing light
My heart is now healthy and beating

My Lord has made me whole again
My post-operative Care
Is forever too praise
My Lord, God in Jesus name

Kari Thomason and Alan Kemp

Psalm 73:26

My flesh and my heart may fail, but God is the strength of my heart and
my portion forever.

Brick By Brick

I started building my wall
At the tender age of five
My confusion was my foundation
My tears, my cement
It was to keep me alive
On my hands and knees
In my mind, I searched
The first brick Had to be just right
Not just any brick
Now new like on a building site
It had to be chipped, used reliable
A life time it had to last
To protect me in the
Present, future and hide the past
Through the years
My wall did grow
Solid foundation and cement
Why didn't someone know?
They chipped and chipped
Trying to break through
But they didn't have the right tools
My wall just grew and grew
40 years of medication
Electric Shock treatment
Then along came an Angel
Her first words
I will never forget
"With me I have a wheelbarrow

For every brick you let"
GO
Brick by brick
My wall came down
The pain, confusion and fear
Very slowly, it took a long time
But HEY, I'm still here

<u>Don't Give Up</u>

You used me and abused me
But you will never know
The strength I built within me
To let the whole world know
That's it you who the weak ones
The evil and the bad
It may have taken me A lot of years
But I am no longer sad
I wear the scars
I have shed the tears
My hurting I have done
But I have something
You never had
The love of a Special Someone
God has always travelled with me
He never left my side
Many times, I thought
He had abandoned me
Because I was a damaged child
No, it's you who were the damaged ones
With pure Evil in your hearts
When you used me and abused me?
My spirit would depart
To a special place
Where there was no pain
Where I knew I was loved
In God's arms, that held me tight
Until the Evil deed was done

And here I am
To tell the world

And tell the world I will
To reach the ears and hearts of everyone
Especially the young
God is there; he's not abandoned you
The pain He will make numb
And those bad and evil ones
Their hearts will come undone
Please don't give up Little Ones
He his right there by your side
Whether your 6 or 56 years old
He'll wipe the tears you hide
He will never leave you
Your hand he'll always hold
Because you are SPECIAL
With a story to be told

Kari Thomason/Kaleidoscope

<u>A Bloody Good Moan</u>

I guess from the title
You're entitled to groan
Yes, I'm at it again
Having a moan
Out of my system
I must get rid of this shite
The only way I know how
Is for me to write
I take a tablet
Only another 7 to go
Hey, that's just breakfast
Dinner, tea and night-time
Still to go though
3 inhalers and nebulisers
The oxygen will be next
"Come on, give me a break".
I am longing to put in a text
Then I remind myself
That the body is just a shell
My mind and my Spirit
Seem to be surviving well
Please don't screw them up
With all your Text Book stuff
My brain is screaming
Enough is enough
Some say my sense of humour
Is as dry as a bone
I'd like to think

I don't always moan
But it all just overwhelmed me
Sending me almost to despair
But I'm feeling tons better
Thanks guys for being there

My Plea

I am putting myself up for adoption
No teeth, but a big cheeky grin
I don't eat much, I am toilet trained
Rather plum instead of thin
A wicked sense of humour
You've probably guessed that by now?
Reading this, I bet you're thinking
Kari, you're one crazy cow!!!
See what loneliness does to you?
Around an empty house I roam
No kids cluttering up the place
Long ago, from the nest they have flown
Just sit me in corner
I won't put up much of a fight
All that I would ask for
Is pens and paper to write
I'm a very good listener
And have a lot of love to give
Don't worry it wouldn't be long term
Only, as long as I live
So far, there have been no takers
Oh, actually there is one
Who has no special requirements!
Who accepts, just the way I am

Kari Thomason/Kaleidoscope

The deal is definitely done
God has been with me from the start
And will be at the End
How can I be lonely?
When God, is my best friend?

Peace

Is this powerful feeling
Really for keeps?
In fact, is it going to last?
Can it be trusted
Or will it let me down?
As often, my feelings have in the past
Is it new? Have I had it before?
A difficult one to tell
I have had my share
Of highs and Lows
This is different, strange as well
Strange, but in a beautiful way
Calming, soothing.... nice
That's why I'm asking
Is this for keeps?
I know, I've asked that twice
Perhaps, I'm afraid to find out
What if it really isn't keeps?
I must shake off this doubt
I must trust my instincts
I must trust my heart
I must trust God, who
Has been with me from the start
God, who with open arms   accepted me
Giving me all the Love, that I seek
Also, the answer to my question
YES, this is for keeps

Daughter

The scene in front of me
Brings a tear to my eye
Journeying me back
To when you were five
A question you used to ask me
"Mummy, why are you so sad?"
Dolly and I, we want to make you glad
Daddy says, your new medicines
Makes you feel really bad
I thought they'd make you happy
Why are you still sad?
Please use my pennies
Then you can buy your 'pop'
And we can sing, dance and laugh
We won't stop
Please don't go to hospital
And leave us alone
Mr. Sunshine stays away
Until you come home
I know that you love writing
Can't you write me a letter?
Tell me everything that makes you sad
So, Dolly and I can make it better

Now I'm watching you
With your youngest on your knee
Tearfully telling you the story
Of how he hurt his knee

"Look Nana, I'm all better now
With Mummy's magic kiss
Did you see it bleed, Nana?
Wow! As big as this......"
We both exchanged smiles
Each with thoughts of our own
Long, long ago memories
Oh, how the years have flown
"You okay Mum, you look sad?"
Had she tuned in to the thoughts
I'd just had?
"Did I have magic kisses?
That worked this good?"
"Of course, you did Mum,
Sometimes better than they should...."

Love Mum xxx

<u>Pausing A Moment</u>

I am sitting in my kitchen/
Office, whatever
Staring out of the window
At the gloomy weather
Weighing up my mood
As I put the kettle on
Down to my last latte
My tea bags are all gone
My electric, on emergency
A sad state of affairs
Come on ask me the question
"Do I really care?"
My body is weary
But at least I'm alive
Ok, going through a bit
Of trouble and strife
Good days, bad days
All part of life's plan
You just have to get through it
The best way you can
Having a family that love me
And friendships that are true
Makes me a very RICH person
Because I have all of you

Thank you

If your day is gloomy.......switch a light on

<u>Nana Duty</u>

What is a Nana's duty?
What can they expect?
Should we start a rulebook?
So, neither one forgets
Lots of babysitting
That's probably rule number 1
She should have "Mary Poppins' powers
To make it lots of fun
Lots of special kisses
To take away all pain
Open arms, and big hugs
To make you feel safe again
A kind ear, without an earring
Nothing must get in the way
When sharing all of your secrets
Your secrets with Nana are safe
A smile that only Nanas' have
Even sometimes when she's sad
You know that she is weary
And her bones are aching like mad
You know she should be going home
Yet, an extra story she will read
Helping you tidy up your stuff
When there really is no need

Your Nana never had a Nana
But this one sure sounds fun
So, Ben and Max and Phoenix
I promise to abide by these rules
Ummm I'm not sure about rule number 1

Love Nana xxx

<u>Chasing A Rainbow</u>

I am chasing a rainbow
What does it mean?
A totally, impossible
Far-fetched dream?
I am chasing a rainbow
The colours make
My heart melts
Like a snowflake on the tongue
Oh, it's so heartfelt
I am chasing a rainbow
I am in no rush
Why wait for a downpour?
The wind can give it a gentle nudge
I am chasing a rainbow
I have no fear
Its beauty lets me know
That God Is near

<u>Not The End</u>

I watched the Consultant
Shaking his head
He gave a deep sigh
These words he said
"The news isn't good
That, you may have guessed?"
Searching for words,
I stopped him and said
"Errr, hold it right there
Don't say another word
Yes, some of it I've guessed
Some of it I've overheard
I don't intend going anywhere
At least not yet
My heart and lungs maybe knackered
But there is life in me yet
I may not have the stamina
For a night on the town
Neither have I the intention
Of wallowing around
I have too much to see
Even more to do
Following no medical Journals
Properly, breaking all the rules
Do you think I am angry?
Do you think I am sad?
Do you think I am delusional?
Do you think I am Clinically Mad?

What I am, is on a Mission
To get things done
A Mission that includes EVERYONE
All those that have hurt me
My forgiveness is there
All those that love me
My heartfelt thanks I share
No more Clinic appointments
New medications, no more
Yes, I know the outcome
I know the score
Hey Doc, don't look so glum
This isn't the end
But a new beautiful beginning
With a very dear FRIEND

A Pep Talk

Lord can we have
One of our chats?
Nothing too serious
You know, just this and that
Some time on our own
Just you and me
They are a great comfort to me
I'm concerned I am not praying hard enough
Don't mistake this for doubting
Your Eternal Love
Maybe I'm making
Too many demands
Requests....... hopes?
I worry sometimes
You find it difficult to cope?
Maybe I don't thank you enough
For each answered prayer?
I know I'm guilty of that one
Much to my despair
I know sometimes I get negative
I'm working on that one
Trying hard not to undo
Everything you have done
Well thanks for the chat Lord

I guess I'll get going
Never doubting
Always knowing
I am your CHILD
Thank you for loving me

ABOUT THE AUTHOR
Kari Thomason

Kari Thomason is an English poet, and has been writing poetry for over 40 years. Most of her work is based on her personal journey through life, all the good, the bad and the ugly!

She was born, raised and has lived in Leeds, England, most of her life, with the exception of living in Scotland and Norfolk for a few years in between. Kari became a member of a Facebook group called Poetry In Motion (PIMs for short) and after uploading some of her poems, she went on to win the highly acclaimed Honouree Golden Pen award, an award that had never been won in the group before. A few months later, she won another award on PIMs, A Silver in Wildfire Publications, which resulted in 12 of her poems narrated and uploaded onto YouTube, 5 of which have gone global, her own webpage, and 4 poems will be published in a book that is coming out at Christmas (2017).

It is from this that has got her work noticed, and has had lots of interest from writers/companies all around the world.

Kari is a mum of 2, with 3 grandchildren, who are her absolute world. Due to ill health, she spends her days at home, concentrating on her poetry, and has recently become a born-again Christian, and enjoys going to church, and meeting fellow Christians. Kari is now also known as a Christian poet.